Life Cycles

Frog

Louise Spilsbury

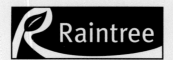

Raintree

www.raintreepublishers.co.uk
Visit our website to find out more information about **Raintree** books.

To order:
☎ Phone 44 (0) 1865 888112
▤ Send a fax to 44 (0) 1865 314091
▢ Visit the Raintree Bookshop at **raintreepublishers.co.uk** to browse our catalogue and order online.

First published in Great Britain by Raintree, Halley Court, Jordan Hill, Oxford OX2 8EJ, part of Harcourt Education.
Raintree is a registered trademark of Harcourt Education Ltd.

Editorial: Charlotte Guillain and Diyan Leake
Design: Michelle Lisseter
Picture Research: Maria Joannou and Debra Weatherley
Production: Lorraine Hicks

Originated by Dot Gradations
Printed and bound in China by South China Printing Company

ISBN 1 844 21250 5 (hardback)
07 06 05 04
10 9 8 7 6 5 4 3 2

ISBN 1 844 21255 6 (paperback)
08 07 06 05 04
10 9 8 7 6 5 4 3 2 1

British Library Cataloguing in Publication Data
Spilsbury, Louise
Frog
571.8'1789
A full catalogue record for this book is available from the British Library.

Acknowledgements
The publishers would like to thank the following for permission to reproduce photographs: Ardea pp. 7 (Ian Beames), **10** (John Mason); Bruce Coleman pp. 16 (Jane Burton), 17 (Kim Taylor), 20 (M.P.L. Fogden), 23 (webbed feet, M.P.L. Fogden); Ecoscene (Anthony Cooper) pp. 6, 23 (female, lay); FLPA pp. 4 (C. Newton), 5 (Martin B. Withers), 9 (Foto Natura Stock), 18 (Jurgen & Christine Sohns), 23 (hatch, Foto Natura Stock); Getty Images p. 21 (Stone); Nature Picture Library p. 19 (Nick Garbutt); NHPA p. 8 (Stephen Dalton); Oxford Scientific Films pp. 12, 13, 23 (insects, Robert Parks); Papilio pp. 14 (Robert Pickett), 15 (Robert Pickett), 22 (Clive Druett), back cover (webbed feet, Clive Druett); Science Photo Library (Gusto) pp. 11, back cover (tadpoles)

Cover photograph of a frog, reproduced with permission of Ardea (John Daniels)

Every effort has been made to contact copyright holders of any material reproduced in this book. Any omissions will be rectified in subsequent printings if notice is given to the publishers.

Contents

Some words are shown in bold, **like this**. They are explained in the glossary on page 23.

What is a frog?

This is a frog.

Frogs are small animals that can live on land and in water.

Frogs start life underwater.

A frog starts life inside an egg.

Where do frogs lay eggs?

Female frogs **lay** eggs in water.

They lay hundreds of eggs at a time.

The eggs are covered in a kind of jelly.

The eggs are called frog spawn.

What are frogs' eggs like?

These are a frog's eggs.

The black shape inside each egg will grow into a young frog.

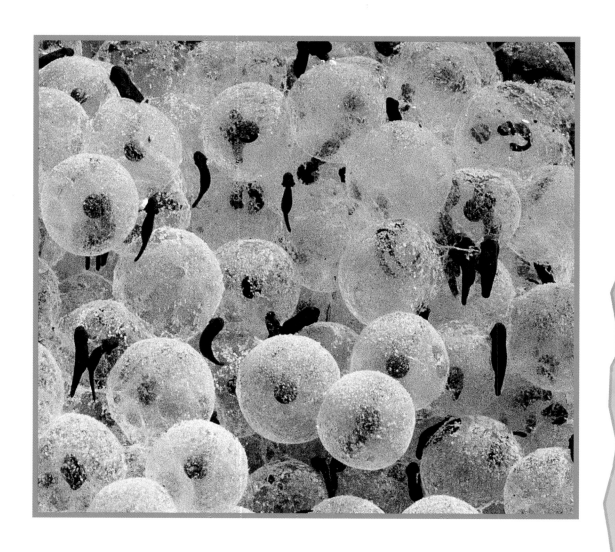

Tadpoles **hatch** out of the eggs.

Tadpoles are young frogs.

What are tadpoles like?

Each tadpole has a long tail.

Tadpoles use their tail
for swimming.

Tadpoles eat plants.

They scrape off bits of plant with tiny teeth.

When do tadpoles grow legs?

When the tadpole is 2 months old it has back legs.

Its body is long.

The tadpoles use their legs to swim faster.

When do tadpoles become frogs?

At 9 weeks old the tadpole grows front legs.

Now it looks more like a little frog.

Then the tail gets much smaller.

The young frog leaves the water when it is 4 months old.

What do frogs eat?

Frogs eat flies and other **insects**.

They also eat worms and spiders.

Frogs jump to catch insects.

Their long back legs help them to jump high.

How do frogs keep safe?

Some animals like to eat frogs.

Bats and some birds eat frogs.

Frogs come out at night.

It is harder for other animals
to catch them at night.

Where do frogs live?

Frogs like to live in damp places on land.

They live near ponds or among plants.

Frogs have **webbed feet** to help them swim.

They go back into water to **lay** eggs of their own.

Frog map

head

eyes

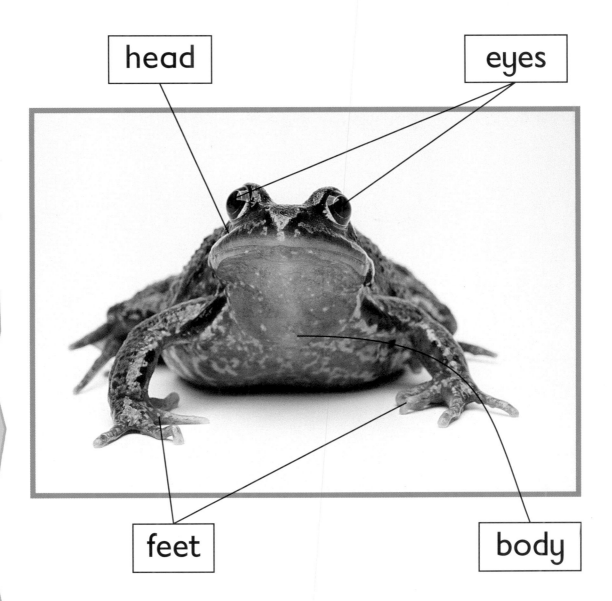

feet

body

Glossary

 **female** female animals can have babies or lay eggs that hatch into babies

 **hatch** come out of an egg

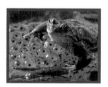 **insects** small animals that have six legs. Butterflies and beetles are kinds of insects.

 **lay** when an egg comes out of an animal's body

 **webbed feet** animal feet that have skin between the toes

Index